Bible reflections
for older people

BRF

The Bible Reading Fellowship
15 The Chambers, Vineyard
Abingdon OX14 3FE
brf.org.uk

The Bible Reading Fellowship (BRF) is a Registered Charity (233280)

ISBN 978 0 85746 618 1
All rights reserved

Acknowledgements
Scripture quotations from The New Revised Standard Version of the Bible, Anglicised edition, copyright © 1989, 1995 by the Division of Christian Education of the National Council of the Churches of Christ in the United States of America. Used by permission. All rights reserved.

Extracts from the Authorised Version of the Bible (The King James Bible), the rights in which are vested in the Crown, are reproduced by permission of the Crown's Patentee, Cambridge University Press.

Scripture quotations taken from The Holy Bible, New International Version (Anglicised edition) copyright © 1979, 1984, 2011 by Biblica. Used by permission of Hodder & Stoughton Publishers, a Hachette UK company. All rights reserved. 'NIV' is a registered trademark of Biblica. UK trademark number 1448790.

Scripture quotations taken from the Holy Bible, New Living Translation, copyright © 1996, 2004, 2007, 2013. Used by permission of Tyndale House Publishers, Inc., Carol Stream, Illinois 60188. All rights reserved.

Scripture quotations are taken from THE MESSAGE, copyright © 1993, 1994, 1995, 1996, 2000, 2001, 2002 by Eugene H. Peterson. Used by permission of NavPress. All rights reserved. Represented by Tyndale House Publishers, Inc.

'Many Blessings' on p. 34 © 2016, Bernard Thorogood, The United Reformed Church. Used with permission.

Every effort has been made to trace and contact copyright owners for material used in this resource. We apologise for any inadvertent omissions or errors, and would ask those concerned to contact us so that full acknowledgement can be made in the future.

A catalogue record for this book is available from the British Library

Printed and bound by CPI Group (UK) Ltd, Croydon CR0 4YY

Contents

About the writers

David Winter is one of BRF's most popular writers. Formerly producer and Head of Religious Broadcasting at the BBC, he is also the author of 43 books, the most recent being *Heaven's Morning: Rethinking the destination* (BRF, 2016). Now retired from full-time ministry, he lives in Berkshire.

Heather Pencavel is a writer new to BRF. A retired minister in the United Reformed Church, she worked in Industrial Chaplaincy in Bristol and later edited the national monthly magazine of the Industrial Mission Association. Heather's passion is writing, and she has written poems, prayers and reflections for various anthologies. She is married to Robin and has four daughters, twin granddaughters and a rescue dog, Bobby.

Tony Horsfall has been a missionary and pastor, and now travels widely, speaking and leading retreats. He is an experienced mentor and has a special concern for spiritual growth as people journey through life and into maturity. He has written eight books for BRF, including *Rhythms of Grace* (2012), *Deep Calls to Deep* (2015), and his latest, a booklet called *Facing Midlife* (2017).

Lin Ball's career began in journalism over 40 years ago. Highlights include interviewing missionaries for OMF, editing Bible resources with Scripture Union for over twelve years, creating radio programmes about disability, and helping a friend write and publish his story weeks before cancer claimed his earthly life.

From the Editor

Welcome to this new collection of Bible reflections.

I love the idea that everyone in the world is connected by six links – the so-called 'six degrees of separation' – and when links emerge between the people I know and meet, it always makes me pause to appreciate the mysterious interconnectedness of our world.

I've had a lot of those moments since beginning to work on these reflections. People I knew many years ago have come back into my life and I'm meeting new people every day. A hidden network of overlapping friends and colleagues has become visible.

This happens not just with people, but with ideas and preoccupations. That phrase 'there's something in the air' captures it well. So it is, here in these reflections. Two writers, quite independently, mention songs by Hank Williams, and as I was reading Tony Horsfall's series on 'living water', an old friend and associate, the theatre director James Roose-Evans, sent me some words from the journal he kept on his ordination retreat in 1981: 'In the chapel here at Glasshampton Monastery, where I spend many hours in prayer, two of the friars are also waiting in the silence to be filled like jugs at a tap until each of us is brim-full, that God may be in us as we are in him. We need continually to go to the tap, or the well, to draw from the eternal spring.'

We do indeed.

God bless you

Using these reflections

Perhaps you have always had a special daily time for reading the Bible and praying. But now, as you grow older, you are finding it more difficult to keep to a regular pattern or find it hard to concentrate. Or maybe you've never done this before. Whatever your situation, these Bible reflections aim to help you take a few moments to read God's word and pray, whenever you are able.

When to read them

You can read these Bible reflections in the morning or last thing at night, or any time during the day. Why not use them as a way of making 'an appointment to be with God'?

There are 40 daily Bible reflections, grouped around four themes. Each one includes some verses from the Bible, a reflection to help you in your own thinking about God and a suggestion for prayer. The reflections aren't dated, so it doesn't matter if you're not able to read them every day. The Bible verses are printed, but if you'd like to read from your own Bible, that's fine too.

How to read them

- **Take time** to quieten yourself, becoming aware of God's presence, asking him to speak to you through the Bible and the reflection.

- **Read** the Bible verses and the reflection:
  - What do you especially like or find helpful in these verses?
  - What might God be saying to you through this reading?
  - Is there something to pray about or thank God for?

- **Pray**. Each reflection includes a prayer suggestion. You might like to pray for yourself or take the opportunity to think about and pray for others.

The thankful life

David Winter

'Say thank you to Grandma' – that was probably the first command we were given, when we were about two. Saying 'thank you' is a necessary courtesy of life, but actually being thankful is much more than that. It's a key element of the truly fulfilled life.

When we think of people we have known and admired for their inner serenity and sense of joy, invariably a key part of their character has been this precious gift of gratitude. An elderly friend who died recently had narrowly survived the war-time blitz in London, lost her first husband, a soldier, a year after they married, had two grown-up daughters who died before reaching 40 and finally lost her second husband. What, you might ask, did she have to be 'thankful' for? Yet at her funeral the repeated theme was the joy expressed in her characteristic sense of gratitude. It was a wonderful reminder that an 'attitude of gratitude' can transform darkness into light.

Of course, life has its dark moments – the 'valley of the shadow'. The Bible, and our experience, tell us that it is not 'roses, roses all the way'. But life itself is gift, in all its glorious complexity. So is fun and laughter, music, the garden, the beauty of nature and the surpassing joy of human love. For the gifts of our Creator-God, gratitude is the only appropriate response.

Psalm 103:1–4 (NRSV)

Remembering the benefits

Bless the Lord, O my soul, and all that is within me, bless his holy name. Bless the Lord, O my soul, and do not forget all his benefits – who forgives all your iniquity, who heals all your diseases, who redeems your life from the Pit, who crowns you with steadfast love and mercy.

This is the Psalmist in full 'thank-you' mode. I don't think he's suggesting that each of us will be healed of all diseases and be saved from death ('the Pit'), but that every time we are healed or delivered from disease or danger, the Lord is the One we should be thanking. God is, he asserts, in the 'blessings' business – they are his 'benefits' for us.

Of course, people still get sick and die – in biblical times and now. But just as sins can be forgiven, so sickness and infirmity can be occasions when we experience the 'steadfast love' that the Psalms so often speak of. Indeed, this 'steadfast love' – sometimes translated as 'loving-kindness' or 'faithful love' – is the absolute hallmark of God's nature. As Paul says: 'Neither death, nor life, nor angels, nor rulers, nor things present, nor things to come, nor powers, nor height, nor depth, nor anything else in all creation, will be able to separate us from the love of God that is in Christ Jesus our Lord' (Romans 8:38–39, NIV).

■ **PRAYER**

Lord, help me not to forget your 'benefits', your 'steadfast love', in the midst of the daily routine and the inevitable setbacks of life. Amen

Psalm 92:1–2, 4 (NRSV)

Morning and night

It is good to give thanks to the LORD, to sing praises to your name, O Most High; to declare your steadfast love in the morning, and your faithfulness by night… For you, O LORD, have made me glad by your work; at the works of your hand I sing for joy.

When 'LORD' is printed in the Bible in capital letters, it means the writer has used the most holy name of God, *Yahweh* – 'I Am'. It is a solemn reminder that God is the unchanging Existing One, the Lord who is simply 'there'.

Here, the psalmist uses that great truth as a kind of structure for the day. In the morning, he wakes up to give thanks and 'sing praises'; in the evening, he reflects on God's 'faithfulness'. All through the events of the day – whatever they have involved – he can recognise that God is present.

'I Am' is never absent, whether we recognise his presence or not. The writer has seen 'the works of his hand' and so he can 'sing for joy'. Now there's a thought as the head hits the pillow – sing a song of praise!

■ PRAYER
Lord, help me to see your hand even in the difficulties and complications of the day, and to be 'made glad' by your faithful care. Amen

Psalm 9:1, 9–10 (NRSV)

In times of trouble

I will give thanks to the Lord with my whole heart; I will tell of all your wonderful deeds… The Lord is a stronghold for the oppressed, a stronghold in times of trouble. And those who know your name put their trust in you, for you, O Lord, have not forsaken those who seek you.

I had a very dear friend and colleague 30 years ago, a Christian minister and broadcaster of rare gifts, who in his early 40s was diagnosed with terminal liver cancer. He told me that one night in bed, he was overwhelmed with a 'horror of great darkness'.

He thought of what lay ahead – his three young children all under ten, his lovely wife, all his hopes for the future dashed. For a moment, the sense of panic was overwhelming. And then it was as though he heard a voice: 'Listen! You've preached to others. Can't you believe it for yourself? I will be with you, whatever lies ahead.'

Then, he told me, a great sense of serenity engulfed him – and stayed with him, as I can testify, all through the two years of advancing weakness until his death. 'I knew,' he said, 'that I would never be abandoned.' I have remembered his words: 'never abandoned'. Isn't that in itself a 'wonderful deed'?

■ PRAYER

Heavenly Father, help me to believe your promise that those who 'know God's name and trust in him' are never abandoned, and be thankful. Amen

Philippians 4:5–7 (NRSV)

The answer to worry

Let your gentleness be known to everyone. The Lord is near. Do not worry about anything, but in everything by prayer and supplication with thanksgiving let your requests be made known to God. And the peace of God, which surpasses all understanding, will guard your hearts and your minds in Christ Jesus.

This is a well-known passage, but as we're thinking about gratitude I feel we can highlight two words: 'with thanksgiving'. We wouldn't naturally associate 'thanksgiving' with prayer in a time of deep worry or anxiety – but there it is, right in the middle of the precious promise of God's help.

We are not being grateful for the problem, whatever it is, but that we have a God to whom we can 'make our requests known'. What an interesting phrase. We don't 'tell' God our worries, but simply let him in on them, as though he's far from reluctant to hear them, but actually waiting to help. As Paul has just said, 'The Lord is near.'

■ PRAYER
As I bring my worries and anxieties to you, Lord, give me a grateful heart, recognising the blessing of a heavenly Father with whom I can share them – and the peace which you alone can give. Amen

2 Corinthians 9:7, 11–12 (NRSV)

Gratitude is infectious

Each of you must give as you have made up your mind, not reluctantly or under compulsion, for God loves a cheerful giver… You will be enriched in every way for your great generosity, which will produce thanksgiving to God through us; for the rendering of this ministry not only supplies the needs of the saints but also overflows with many thanksgivings to God.

This is the apostle Paul on the subject of our giving for the needs of others, in this case, the Christians – 'the saints' – in need in Macedonia.

I know how much some of us worry about this issue. We've perhaps got a little nest egg in the building society, but there are so many desperate needs that are constantly brought to our attention. We can feel guilty or pressurised because we've got it while others are in need.

Here is Paul's advice: give 'as you have made up your mind', not on the spur of the moment or under pressure. But give 'cheerfully', because what you give, however large or small, will not only help to meet a need, but overflow in 'many thanksgivings to God'. This is a triple blessing – to the ones helped, to the cheerful giver and, of course, to God.

■ PRAYER

Help me, Lord, as I consider my Christian giving, to give thoughtfully, cheerfully and thankfully. Amen

1 Thessalonians 5:15–18 (NRSV)

As part of the good life

See that none of you repays evil for evil, but always seek to do good to one another and to all. Rejoice always, pray without ceasing, give thanks in all circumstances; for this is the will of God in Christ Jesus for you.

Paul is reminding the Thessalonians of the hallmarks of the good life. They should seek to 'do good', not just to their fellow Christians but to everybody. They should enjoy their faith, rejoicing in God. They should make prayer their daily breath, ready to place any situation into the hands of God, and 'give thanks in all circumstances'.

Alright. I've just burnt the supper. I've had a fall in the back garden. The car won't start. These are 'circumstances'. How do I turn them into gratitude? The answer to that admittedly hard question must be that as we burnt the supper, or fell in the garden, or tried to start the car, we never moved beyond the boundaries of God's love and care. He is not just with us when life is rosy, but when things go wrong, even badly wrong. Those of us who have experienced God's love and presence during bereavement know the truth of that.

■ **PRAYER**
Lord, help me to see these elements of the good life as God-given steps for me on the narrow road that leads to life. Amen

Luke 17:12–19 (NRSV, abridged)

Words matter

As he entered a village, ten lepers approached [Jesus]… They called out, saying, 'Jesus, Master, have mercy on us!' When he saw them, he said to them, 'Go and show yourselves to the priests.' And as they went, they were made clean. Then one of them, when he saw that he was healed, turned back, praising God with a loud voice. He prostrated himself at Jesus' feet and thanked him. And he was a Samaritan… Then [Jesus] said to him, 'Get up and go on your way; your faith has made you well.'

This story has several messages. The most obvious concerns the Samaritan, 'this foreigner' (v. 18), who, unlike the religiously correct Jews (as they saw themselves), recognised the hand of God in his healing and gave thanks. The second message is that we should not only feel gratitude but say so. I imagine the other nine were also grateful to be cleansed from this disfiguring and isolating condition. But they rushed off without a word.

The third message is that blessing follows every genuine expression of gratitude. The Samaritan praised God and fell at the feet of Jesus in worship. His reward was to be told that he was not only rid of his leprosy, like the others, but was transformed, literally 'made whole'.

■ **PRAYER**

When I feel grateful, Lord, help me to say so, that others may share my blessing. Amen

Colossians 3:14–15 (NRSV)

And be thankful...

Above all, clothe yourselves with love, which binds everything together in perfect harmony. And let the peace of Christ rule in your hearts, to which indeed you were called in the one body. And be thankful.

These words of Paul can help us assess how well our church is fulfilling its calling. The keynotes are three words: love, peace and gratitude.

Love is to be the gift that 'above all' binds the church together in 'perfect harmony'. Notice, it is harmony, not unison. Unison is like one voice; harmony is many different voices combining to make beautiful music. That is Paul's vision of the church. We are not all the same, and God doesn't want us to be, but he does want a divine harmony to emerge from that productive difference.

'The peace of Christ' is to 'rule' in their hearts. The word translated 'rule' is very close to our word 'referee' – the judge of what is right and wrong. If we truly seek that peace, we shall be able to disagree with our fellow Christians without being disagreeable.

'And be thankful.' There it is again, the inevitable footnote. Love and peace are God's gifts, the 'fruit of the Spirit'. Gratitude for gifts is surely what we've been taught from childhood.

■ PRAYER
Lord, may I and my fellow Christians be filled with your love and peace, and then be thankful for the gift. Amen

Psalm 100:4–5 (NRSV)

Steadfast love

Enter his gates with thanksgiving, and his courts with praise. Give thanks to him, bless his name. For the Lord is good; his steadfast love endures for ever, and his faithfulness to all generations.

One of the loveliest words in Hebrew, the language of the Old Testament, is *chesedh*. Our Bibles offer at least three translations of it, but you will quickly recognise them, because they occur over and again in the Psalms: 'loving-kindness', 'steadfast love' and 'faithful love'. Between them, they seem to me to summarise the very heart of our gratitude to God in all circumstances.

'Loving-kindness' speaks of a warm and affectionate concern, like a reassuring cuddle for a tearful child. 'Steadfast love' speaks of a love that doesn't change, which is why we can speak of God's 'eternal' love. This is a love that endures for ever. Then 'faithful love' speaks of a love that remains true whatever is happening around us (or within us), that never lets us down or leaves us in the lurch.

Over and over again, the psalmists sing of God's *chesedh*, and this is what they mean: a love that is gentle, reliable and utterly faithful.

■ **PRAYER**

Help me today, Lord, to come into your presence with praise and thanksgiving for this 'steadfast love that endures for ever'. Amen

Colossians 3:16–17 (NRSV)

Whatever you do

Let the word of Christ dwell in you richly… and with gratitude in your hearts sing psalms, hymns, and spiritual songs to God. And whatever you do, in word or deed, do everything in the name of the Lord Jesus, giving thanks to God the Father through him.

'Whatever,' your teenage grandson might say. Of course, he means, 'Who cares?' But actually, 'whatever' is a very specific word. It is all-encompassing, offering no exceptions. 'Whatever you do', therefore, is an all-inclusive command. Here, the apostle Paul puts it in the setting of Christian discipleship.

The 'word of Christ' – his teaching, his example – is to 'dwell' in us, make its home there. We are to sing with joy and gratitude our songs of worship to God. And then, just to cover any possible exceptions, we get 'whatever'. 'Whatever you do, in word or deed' is to be done 'in the name of the Lord Jesus'. There is the crucial test. Can I say this word, take this action, spend this money, 'in the sacred name'?

You won't be surprised, either, that all of this is to be done with 'gratitude', 'giving thanks to the Father'. We are to seek to live the thankful life.

■ PRAYER

Thank you, Lord, for the 'word of Christ'. Thank you for our songs and hymns of worship. And may all my life – whatever – be lived 'in the name of the Lord Jesus'. Amen

Gathering light

Heather Pencavel

Most mornings I hear the news on Radio 4. Some mornings, I wish I hadn't – impending conflict, divided communities, economic gloom and diminishing resources. A single news bulletin can cast a long shadow over the day.

On gloomy days, I remember something Archbishop Desmond Tutu said: 'Hope is being able to see that there is light despite all of the darkness.' Light is the first gift given to the newly created universe. It shines in the pages of the Bible from Genesis to Revelation, from first to last.

Light shines through our human story, from our birth to the
   very end:
Light greets us at our birth, that we may grow and thrive
Light shines before us to show us the way
Light shines on our path, that we may walk safely
Light shines above us to lift our eyes from the ground
Light shines for us even when we cannot see
Light shines upon us that we may be seen
Light shines within us to light the way for others
Light shines in others that they may be Christ to us
Light shines at the end that we may know God
who is our beginning, our constant guide
and our welcome at the last.

Genesis 1:1–3 (NRSV)

Dawning light

In the beginning when God created the heavens and the earth, the earth was a formless void and darkness covered the face of the deep, while a wind from God swept over the face of the waters. Then God said, 'Let there be light'; and there was light.

There it was, the new-made universe: the heavens and the earth, formless, empty and dark. Mystery engulfed it as the wind swirled and howled above the water. Then God spoke, and the first light dawned.

The ancient story reflects the light of the experience of God's people over many years of living and learning, in good times and bad, including long years of exile from their homeland. They knew that God speaks into the chaos. They knew that darkness is powerful, but they knew also that God is the source of all things, creator of day as well as night, holder of all things in balance, lover of all.

As we think about our own times, when so much around us is changing, and what once seemed clear and lasting is suddenly insecure, we can know that God still speaks and calls light out of darkness. Someone I once knew used to say, of new ideas, 'It never dawned on me till now!'

■ PRAYER

God, Maker and Lover of all, your light dawns on us in the beauty of a garden, in the eyes of a child, as we read the Bible and in our conversations, in the words of poets, in music and song, and it is very good. Amen

Numbers 6:24–26 (NRSV)

Sharing the light

The Lord bless you and keep you; the Lord make his face to shine upon you and be gracious to you; the Lord lift up his countenance upon you, and give you peace.

When we bless people at their baptism with these words, I remember that we used to say them every night to our children when they were tucked into bed. Once, asked how she had enjoyed her first Brownie camp, one of them said, 'It was good – except… it was dark… and nobody said my blessing.'

This blessing was included in the book of Numbers around 500 years BC. Its words have long comforted God's people, a reminder that God is still and always with us, and his face shines upon us. The Hebrew word translated 'face' means 'presence' or 'whole being'. God is not a distant light or a passing smile, but present in human life, and God's presence is protection and peace.

At worship in the synagogue, Jesus saw the priest raise his hands and bless the people with these words. He heard them during the sabbath meal; they were part of his world, as they are part of ours. May we hold them close and share them widely with all who wait in the dark for someone to bless them.

■ PRAYER
Loving God, when I am alone in the dark, open my eyes to your light, shared in the kindness of friends and strangers, and give me peace. Amen

Job 29:1–3 (NRSV)

Walking in the dark

[Job] said: 'O that I were as in the months of old, as in the days when God watched over me; when his lamp shone over my head, and by his light I walked through darkness.'

When things go wrong, it is natural to remember the past. We wish we were back there in the days when everything was, if not wonderful, better than it is now. So did Job. Ageing, ill, impoverished, bereaved and surrounded by 'friends' insisting that he must somehow be to blame for it all, he had good cause to long for past times. Remembering 'the friendship of God' he once enjoyed, Job assumes that it is now ended. God is absent, the darkness overwhelming. Why has this happened? He doesn't deserve this. He is not angry, but sad and bewildered.

There have been dark times before. Job recognises that God's light has guided him in the past. But that was then: 'I was in my prime. Now – look at me: God-forsaken.' In his depressed state, Job can't see it, but the light still shines and, eventually, remembering God's past faithfulness helps him to encounter God again and renew his trust.

■ **PRAYER**

I give thanks for happy memories, and the blessings of past times. When I can't see the way forward, help me to remember, and to remind others, that your light will never fail. Amen

Isaiah 9:2, 6a (NRSV)

Darkness to light

The people who walked in darkness have seen a great light; those who lived in a land of deep darkness – on them light has shined… For a child has been born for us, a son given to us.

'For unto us a child is born…' I can hear Handel's music in my head as I write. Isaiah's song offers hope: light instead of darkness, peace and justice instead of fear and oppression.

For Isaiah, 'the people who lived in a land of deep darkness' meant victims of the Assyrian occupation of Israel. Still, today, we know of countries where people live in poverty, oppression and fear, or are forced to flee for their lives.

Isaiah believed that the Assyrians would be defeated and a new king would rise up and bring lasting peace and justice – this is the child, the son who is given. Jewish people hear these words and think with hope of a messianic age, yet to come. Christians, beginning with Matthew (4:12–16), understand the words to refer to Jesus, light of the world.

So, what can we who follow Jesus do today to let God's light of hope, peace and justice shine in the world through us, wherever we are?

■ **PRAYER**

We pray for victims of war and terrorism, of injustice and rejection; for those who live in constant fear; and for all who flee famine or persecution: may they find peace, healing and welcome. Amen

Psalm 18:28–29; Psalm 119:105 (NRSV)

Walking in the light

It is you who light my lamp; the Lord, my God, lights up my darkness. By you I can crush a troop, and by my God I can leap over a wall… Your word is a lamp to my feet and a light to my path.

Walking in God's light seems like an energetic business. It's been a while since I climbed over a wall. David was a young man, a soldier, and this psalm was written 'on the day when the Lord delivered him from the hand of all his enemies'. He had every reason for energetic and enthusiastic thanksgiving.

We may not be called to – or fit for – physical fighting or wall-climbing, but we have a path to walk in our lives every day: decisions to make, tasks to do and people to meet. If, like me, you are finding retirement busy just now, you may be wondering where to find the energy and where it will all end. When we look to God's word to light our lamp and lighten our darkness, we discover that the light will shine in two places: a light above us to give us direction, and light for our feet to show where the next step should be. I just need there to be no walls to climb!

■ **PRAYER**

Help me, God of love, to look for your light in the Bible, in the stories of faith and the wisdom of prophets. Give me strength and courage to walk your way, one step at a time. Amen

John 1:9–12 (NRSV, abridged)

Light of the world

The true light… was coming into the world… Yet the world did not know him… and his own people did not accept him. But to all who received him, who believed in his name, he gave power to become children of God.

There's an old song by Hank Williams that goes: 'Jesus came like a stranger in the night. Praise the Lord, I saw the light!'

Jesus, light of the world, came into the world a stranger to his own people. They knew the carpenter's son turned storyteller, healer and travelling preacher. But very few saw the light. Most just saw a short life which ended in a cruel death.

For centuries, people have longed for someone to save them from their oppressors, and bring justice and peace. Jesus didn't overthrow the Romans. He spent time with fishermen, tax collectors and lepers, listening to their stories and healing their bodies and minds. Then he challenged the way things were and was crucified. He wasn't the messiah people were expecting.

Peace and justice start at the grass roots – understanding what is happening to people, hearing their stories and giving them help and hope that things can be better. We can often follow this up by speaking truth to those in power, and asking for change. That's the true light at work. Those who welcome the light and believe in its power are children of God.

■ PRAYER

We give thanks for the light that shines every day in people who take the time to listen to the stories of those who are ignored and bring them to light. Amen

Matthew 5:14–16 (NRSV, abridged)

People of the light

You are the light of the world… No one after lighting a lamp puts it under the bushel basket, but on the lampstand, and it gives light to all in the house. In the same way, let your light shine before others.

I can just remember oil lamps at home, used when there was a power cut. Ours was dim and difficult to light. Once lit, it stayed lit – we certainly didn't cover it up. Its light didn't reach the corners of the room, but it was better than the dark.

But shine too bright a light in the shadows and we find things we don't know how to deal with. We worry about our children's jobs, our grandchildren's future in a world of debt and zero-hours contracts; our own future as health and care provision becomes ever more stretched. We weep at the plight of refugees.

These are things we can't tackle on our own and it's easy to feel helpless. But we can listen, we can pray, we can give, and we can encourage others. We can help to light the world with love and hope and healing. In uncertain times, the light of Christ is needed more than ever. It will never fail, so let it shine for others and for the glory of God.

■ **PRAYER**

God, your light comforts me and challenges me, and sometimes it scares me. Hold me in your hands, as I would hold a candle, and keep my flame strong. Amen

26

Ephesians 5:8–14 (NRSV, abridged)

Reflecting the light

Live as children of light – for the fruit of the light is found in all that is good and right and true... Take no part in the unfruitful works of darkness, but instead expose them... Everything exposed by the light becomes visible, for everything that becomes visible is light.

This summer, we spent a sunny day exploring Canary Wharf, recalling how the area looked when it was just Docklands. I remembered an unforgettable visit a few years ago to the top floor of One Canada Square, then the tallest building in the UK, with a stunning view of London in every direction. Later, waiting for a bus, I noticed an odd thing: above us, the sun was shining on the west-facing glass walls of the surrounding skyscrapers. The glass was reflecting the light to the glass-covered buildings opposite and light was all around.

So it is in these verses from Ephesians: God's light reflected in God's people makes the 'works of darkness' clear and turns darkness into light. Followers of Jesus, 'children of light', are called to look for what is good, and expose the things that damage people, in order to bring change and healing. A small local church I know – most members retired – runs a Memory Café for people with dementia and their carers; ecumenically they support a food bank and sell Traidcraft goods, reflecting God's light in practical ways.

■ **PRAYER**

God of life and love, show me every day how to reflect your light in practical ways in my church and community. Amen

John 1:1–5 (KJV, abridged)

The light shines on

In the beginning was the Word and the Word was with God, and the Word was God… All things were made by him… In him was life, and the life was the light of men. And the light shineth in darkness; and the darkness comprehended it not.

Children in Ulster in my childhood years had no excuse for not knowing the Bible. Many went to church schools, and most were taken to church and/or to afternoon Sunday School. Every week, there were verses from the Authorised Version (KJV) to learn by heart. I find words fascinating, so I enjoyed the experience. Others did not. For some, memorising was hard, understanding even harder.

I chose the Authorised Version for this reading especially for verse 5. Modern translations say, 'The darkness did not *overcome* the light', giving the idea of a continuing battle between light and darkness. Early translators said '*comprehend*', which holds the two ideas of 'understand' and 'encompass'. Light can shine in darkness, but the darkness does not understand it, nor can it encompass it.

When Jesus travelled around Galilee, talking to people, hearing their stories and meeting their needs, those in power didn't understand it and felt threatened. Eventually, they killed him. But still he lives, by his Spirit, in those who follow him – because the other translation works too: 'The light shines in the darkness, and the darkness did not overcome it' (NRSV).

■ PRAYER

When darkness threatens me, remind me that it cannot encompass me; when I feel defeated, remind me that your light cannot be overcome. Amen

Revelation 21:23–24; 22:5 (NRSV, abridged)

Everlasting light

The city has no need of sun or moon to shine on it, for the glory of God is its light... The nations will walk by its light... They need no light of lamp or sun, for the Lord God will be their light and they will reign for ever and ever.

I love a really sunny day: clear blue sky and the occasional white cloud, trees making lacy patterns on the grass, birds taking dust baths and sleepy cats basking in the sun. Or a starlit winter night, when the whole dancing universe is alight with beauty and 'the world is charged with the glory of God.'*

In John's vision, the city of God has no sunny days, no glorious starry nights. Day and night are not needed, for the city is lit by the glory of God. God lives with people and everyone lives in God's light, even the nations, the one-time oppressors of the innocent.

As we let our light shine in whatever ways we can, we know that no one is beyond the love of God. God's light shines for everyone and will never fail. If we feel frustrated that we can no longer be as active as we used to be, we may recall that light doesn't need to be constantly on the move. Streetlights don't move, but they are indispensable.

■ **PRAYER**

Let your Light shine on me today, and help me to light the way for others until your Kingdom of Love will come on earth, as it is in heaven. Amen

* Gerard Manley Hopkins, *God's Grandeur* (1877)

The Gift of Years

Debbie Thrower founded and leads The Gift of Years programme. She has pioneered the Anna Chaplaincy model, offering spiritual care to older people, and is widely involved in training and advocacy. Visit **thegiftofyears.org.uk** to find out more.

Debbie writes…

Welcome, and I hope you enjoy this fresh set of reflections!

Do you remember the No. 1 hit 'Where do you go to (my lovely)?' by Peter Sarstedt? It topped the charts for several weeks in 1969. The singer-songwriter imagined where his love went to in her head when she was alone in her bed…

These reflections are an aid to the imagination, a means of exploring the treasures of our memories. Not all our recollections are happy ones, and the question of what we do with our hurts in later life, especially when we spend more time on our own, is a relevant one.

Our writers have all interpreted the request to draw on passages from the Bible which bring comfort to us in older age in very different ways. Some thoughts may dog us in the dark watches of the night; others will be joyful ones to nourish and sustain us. Whatever may assail us, my hope is that we can welcome our thought-life with the passage of years and be assured of God's welcome when one day he calls us home.

Best wishes

Meet the writer: Heather Pencavel

Heather Pencavel was brought up in the small County Down town of Banbridge, just off the main Belfast to Dublin road. It was a mainly Protestant town, though it did have a Catholic population big enough for there to be a Catholic primary school and secondary school. But, she explains:

The big thing in my life wasn't religion but education – education in the sense of teachers who could see a child with some ability, despite living in a house with only eight books in it. So I got enormous encouragement from teachers. They helped me prepare for the 11+, or 'Qualifying' as it was called in Northern Ireland, and get into grammar school where the teachers were equally supportive and encouraged me all the way through to university entrance when I got into Queen's, Belfast to read French and German.

So was university the big liberation that it often is?

It was a big liberation, yes, though it sounds very sheltered now. In my first year I lived in the 'Presbyterian Hostel', which was mixed, not just for girls, so that was good, and you got three square meals a day and a room of your own for £2.15s a week, which was doable on a student grant.

What happened to your faith journey while you were at university?

Most of my friends were evangelical Christians, including my closest friend, even though we argued all the time. It sounds so narrow now, but university was a real an eye-opener because you met people like Presbyterians. Of course, there were Presbyterians at school but you never talked about religion, but now because we were* at university you could talk about anything, including religion. Mainly what you discovered, of course, were the similarities rather than the differences.

And after university?

I became a Youth Employment Officer, initially in Belfast. It began with a three-month training course, and at the end of the three months I went to work as a trainee Youth Employment Officer in Omagh, which everyone remembers for the bombing years later, in August 1998. After Omagh, I went on to further training in Kent. I met Robin there and somewhere towards the end of the year we had a day out together. Eleven months later we got married and we moved to London.

How did the call to ministry come?

When I started to think about it, I realised that it had been with me all my life. As a child, my party piece was to preach to people.

Nearly all the good decisions I've made in my life have been done on impulse, so there's something around that means my impulses are usually to be trusted. Marrying Robin was one of them and the other was to do with ministry. I'd begun the Lay Preacher course because I just felt I needed to explore and know more about faith and religion, even though with my background I already knew a lot about the Bible. So I was working as a Lay Preacher, still in training, and I was invited to go to a Synod Vocations Day, and there were all these people there who were thinking seriously about candidating for ministry and by the end of the day I'd made the decision to join them.

But given your four little girls, your training was somewhat unconventional?

I can't remember how long my training took, but it was a lot longer than usual – I had my youngest, Gillian, half way through the Old Testament! But I was eventually ordained in 1992, 25 years ago. Everything has always been one step at a time for me – you know the verse: a lamp for my feet rather than a light for my path.

I was working in secular employment off and on throughout my training and one day I was driving along with the Moderator and he said, 'Well, Heather, you've nearly finished now, so what kind of pulpit would you like to occupy?'

And out of my mouth came a thought I'd not formulated before, which was, 'Michael, I don't want to occupy anybody's pulpit, I want to do something with faith and work.' And to his great credit Michael said, 'Oh, right, I know exactly where you need to go' and pointed me in the direction of Social and Industrial Mission, as it then was, in Bristol. So I went and worked there and had various chaplaincies. The first one was at Nuclear Electric in Bedminster, when they were just about to be closed and nearly everyone was facing redundancy – I learned an awful lot there.

The chaplain's mantra is 'Find out what God is doing and join in'. Over the years I've worked with so many people, whom God was doing things with, and they may not have been religious at all, but they were deeply committed and you joined in with them if it was about justice and peace.

The other really important strand in your being is writing?

I have always written since childhood. I find poetry easier because I can switch my cognitive bit off and let things happen in my head which then spill onto the page. I once said to someone, 'I think God lives in the back of my computer because what comes on to the screen is not something that has been through my brain.' I also run a little writing group in Thornbury URC. I wanted people to be able to access their creative side, but it's also true that people will tell you things in a poem that they would never tell you in conversation, so it's a way to help them go deeper.

Bernard Thorogood

Bernard Thorogood celebrated his 90th birthday in July 2017. Born in East Grinstead, he trained in Scotland for the ministry of the Congregational Church and was appointed by the London Missionary Society in 1952 to serve in the Cook Islands in the South Pacific. In 1970, he became General Secretary of the forerunner of the Council for World Mission and in 1980 he was appointed General Secretary of the United Reformed Church, serving until his retirement in 1992.

He then settled with his wife Joan in Sydney, where he became a minister in the Uniting Church of Australia. Author of 13 books, his latest publication is a delightful collection of poems and prayers entitled *Old Grey Prayers*.

In his Foreword, Bernard writes: 'For most of us old age is a tough journey, as our bodies get less agile, less strong, more tired; tougher yet when the mind and memory begin to falter… I hope you will find something here which strikes a chord with your own experience and helps you to face each day with a moment of prayer.'

Many Blessings

When we remember, it is our delight
that we have seen so many lovely faces –
the face of the green landscape,
the face of the white-capped ocean,
the many faces of dawn and sunset,
and the myriad faces of friends.

And that we have met such joys –
like our first discovery of fine poetry,
and the happy family picnic,
and our choir singing in the Town Hall,
and all those children's cricket games on the beach.

And that we have known such people –
some who gave their lives for freedom,
others who lived with humility and grace,
those who had patience with handicap,
and many who kept the faith.

For all the joys that have enriched us
we are forever grateful, God of gifts and graces.

Bernard Thorogood (used with kind permission)

Come, Let Us Age!

Debbie writes:

When my friend **Wanda Nash** died in 2015, she had been working on her last book called, provisionally, 'Being Old'. Wanda brought the same infectious enthusiasm and curiosity to bear on her own ageing as she brought to everything else in her life and it was a privilege, however poignant, to work with Wanda's daughter Poppy to complete the book. We gathered together Wanda's notes, reflections and excerpts from her personal journals, and called the new book *Come, Let Us Age!* in a deliberate echo of her much-loved earlier work *Come, Let Us Play!*

Transformation was always Wanda's goal. Nothing less. So ageing was, for her, another part of the grand adventure of living. Alongside the inevitable signs of diminishing energy, Wanda saw ageing as an opportunity to embrace and celebrate the fruits of life experience, the wisdom gained from coping with life's trials and tribulations, greater understanding of what it is to be human and, perhaps most important of all, the certainty in her mind that life after death was approaching ever closer.

I hope you'll enjoy this brief extract from Chapter 3, pp. 26–27 of *Come, Let Us Age!* (BRF, 2017):

Would God like an empty space which only he can fill?

As bits of our brain drop off, our wits scamper away like rabbits and immediate memories spatter into nothingness – is this a tragedy or an opportunity?

Can it be an 'exercise' that we can *choose*?
Might it turn into a physical, emotional, spiritual '*good*'?
Clearing a space for our Creator?
Emptying, in order to be refilled by God?

To give him space in this busy and so preoccupied world from which he can operate his own purposes? Maybe it could be something like clearing the loft for modern insulation, which is a deliberate, desirable activity – in spite of the horrendous loss and back-stretching work involved. In place of the fear of growing decrepit; instead of resenting future possibilities like memory loss and being taken 'where you do not want to go' (Jesus' remark to Peter in John 21:18); rather than crying over our lessening ability to 'be useful', we can decide to make a clear area: to become emptied, so God can fill us and take over. And we can do this voluntarily!

Being old need not mean diminishment. It's a new chance to meet new learning curves and become friends with them. Opportunities abound to enliven my skills of patience, of letting go, leaving be, allowing. Things I've just skirted around before can at last become my joy, my standby, my way of getting on with those near me and indeed my very soul. All this simply depends on my willingness to taste their flavour. I no longer have to be there (and everywhere), do that (as well as this), instantly recognise and remember the tales of everyone I meet.

And when my memory fails me, I can happily confess to going through a 'senior moment', because these moments are familiar to all those I spend time with now. They actually form a bond, a point of commonality! They can become times of thanksgiving too: 'Thank God, I didn't mess that one up too badly.' At those times when patience, letting go, leaving be and allowing come smoothly, there can be a new sense of being enfolded and becoming enfolding, and so others (even some unknown and unseen by us) can benefit.

Living water
Tony Horsfall

One of my favourite hymns is 'I heard the voice of Jesus say' by the Scottish minister Horatius Bonar (1808–89). It expresses Christ's invitation for us to come to him and find rest for our souls, and brings together beautifully the longings of the human heart with the power of the gospel to meet our need. The second verse stands out for me:

> *I heard the voice of Jesus say, 'Behold, I freely give*
> *The living water; thirsty one, stoop down, and drink, and live.'*
> *I came to Jesus, and I drank of that life giving stream;*
> *My thirst was quenched, my soul revived, and now I live in him.*

As with the other verses, there is first an invitation and then a response of acceptance.

These are timeless words and they move me as much today as the first time I sang this hymn some 40 years ago. They come to mind now because they sum up the theme of this series of notes on living water.

As you read, you will hear time and again that same invitation to come, and drink, and live. I pray that as you read day-by-day, you will make your own response to Jesus. May your thirst be quenched and your soul revived so you too may live in him.

Psalm 104:10–13 (NIV)

The God who waters the mountains

He makes springs pour water into the ravines; it flows between the mountains. They give water to all the beasts of the field; the wild donkeys quench their thirst. The birds of the sky nest by the waters; they sing among the branches. He waters the mountains from his upper chambers; the land is satisfied by the fruit of his work.

Here in Britain, the weather is a major topic of conversation. Our weather is very changeable and varies from day to day. We listen diligently to the weather forecast, eager to know what lies ahead so we can plan accordingly. Often, we complain about the weather. If it is hot, we wish it were cooler; if it is cold, we wish it were warmer.

One thing we never seem to enjoy is the rain. It spoils many of our outdoor events. Some days we have endless drizzle, a soft fine rain that seems to soak everything and creates a feeling of depression. Since we have little fear of drought, we seldom learn to appreciate the rain.

The psalmist, from the perspective of a dry and dusty land, thinks differently. Rain to him is a gift from God, to be received with thankfulness, for without water no life can survive. Animals, plants and humans all need water to exist. No wonder water is a symbol of the life God offers us.

■ **PRAYER**
Lord, thank you for rain, and the water of life. Amen

John 4:10–11 (NIV)

The gift of God

Jesus answered her, 'If you knew the gift of God and who it is that asks you for a drink, you would have asked him and he would have given you living water.' 'Sir,' the woman said, 'you have nothing to draw with and the well is deep. Where can you get this living water?'

These verses are from a familiar Bible story, the encounter of Jesus with the Samaritan woman at the well of Sychar. They illustrate the humanity of Jesus – he is tired, hungry and thirsty – and his compassion towards a stranger who many Jewish men would have totally ignored.

From asking for a drink for himself, Jesus moves the conversation forwards to speak about the living water he is able to offer. For a moment, the woman is confused, thinking by 'living' water he means that which is free-flowing like a stream rather than that which we can draw from the well.

By living water, Jesus means the life and the love of God, which he alone can give, and which alone can satisfy the yearning of the human heart. This is what the woman needs. All her life, she has been searching for acceptance and love. She is about to discover that the longing in her heart can be satisfied in relationship with God. This is what Jesus offers, and it comes as a gift.

■ **PRAYER**
Lord, thank you for the gift of living water. Amen

Isaiah 12:2–3 (NIV)

The wells of salvation

Surely God is my salvation; I will trust and not be afraid. The Lord, the Lord himself, is my strength and my defence; he has become my salvation. With joy you will draw water from the wells of salvation.

I came to faith in Christ as a fourteen-year-old boy in a little Methodist chapel in the Yorkshire mining village where I grew up. I was conscious of my need for forgiveness and realised Jesus had died on the cross to make that possible. With tears rolling down my cheeks, I responded to the call to receive the free gift of salvation.

That was many years ago now and my understanding of salvation has deepened and matured, but that initial joy remains. The living water that Jesus gives is indeed life-giving and sustaining. The deep needs of the human heart for meaning and purpose, to be loved and to feel secure, find their satisfaction in him.

Every day, we have the privilege of drinking again the water of life from a well that will never run dry. What we discover is that, when we are in relationship with God, we are better equipped to deal with the challenges of life. We can find strength through trusting in God so that even when we are worried or afraid, we still have a song in our hearts.

■ PRAYER
Lord, thank you for your salvation and the gift of joy, even in the midst of worry and fear. Amen

Jeremiah 2:13 (NIV)

Forsaking the spring of living water

My people have committed two sins: they have forsaken me, the spring of living water, and have dug their own cisterns, broken cisterns that cannot hold water.

I enjoyed the sweetest drink of water I have ever tasted during a mission trip to Armenia. We stayed with a local family and their water supply came directly from a mountain spring, so it was pure and fresh. I have never tasted anything so refreshing or satisfying.

Most of us find drinking water a little boring, especially since there are so many exciting alternatives. Children will usually pick fizzy drinks if they have a choice and many adults will opt for tea or coffee, but nothing is as healthy as a drink of plain, pure water.

We all face the temptation to satisfy the longings of our hearts apart from God, and the world offers many alternatives. We may indulge in retail therapy or pleasure-seeking to satisfy the ache within. Perhaps we plan another holiday or immerse ourselves in our favourite soap operas to fill the void inside us, yet the emptiness remains. Such home-made solutions can only offer temporary relief at best. They are broken cisterns.

Jeremiah challenged the people of his day not to forsake the God who alone is the spring of living water. That is a danger we too must avoid.

■ PRAYER

Lord, forgive me for foolishly thinking my deepest needs could be met anywhere else but in you. Amen

John 7:37–39a (NIV)

What an invitation

On the last and greatest day of the festival, Jesus stood and said in a loud voice, 'Let anyone who is thirsty come to me and drink. Whoever believes in me, as scripture has said, rivers of living water will flow from within them.' By this he meant the Spirit, whom those who believed in him were later to receive.

A friend of mine has just been to Buckingham Palace for a garden party. He posted on social media pictures of himself and his wife dressed up for the special occasion along with a snapshot of his invitation card. I must say I did feel a little envious.

In these words, recorded in John's Gospel, Jesus makes an even greater invitation to anyone who feels spiritually thirsty, an invitation not for a select few but for all those willing to respond. The invitation is to come to him and drink the living water which he longs to give. He declares it with a loud voice, hoping that as many as possible will hear and respond.

John adds an important word of explanation for us. When Jesus is talking about the living water, he is actually talking about the gift of the Holy Spirit which would be given at Pentecost. It is the Holy Spirit who makes the life and love of God real in our lives.

■ PRAYER

Lord, I come to drink. Thank you for the work of the Spirit in my life today. Amen

1 Corinthians 12:12–13 (NIV)

Learning to drink

Just as a body, though one, has many parts, but all its many parts form one body, so it is with Christ. For we were all baptised by one Spirit so as to form one body – whether Jews or Gentiles, slave or free—and we were all given the one Spirit to drink.

Now that I have grandchildren, I am re-learning the rudiments of child development. It is fascinating to see them develop basic skills, then graduate to more difficult ones, such as learning to hold a cup and drink for themselves. It can be a little messy at first, but a significant achievement when it happens.

Paul reminds us here that we have been given the Holy Spirit and that we must learn how to drink the living water for ourselves. It is part of our growing up as God's children. So how do we learn to drink?

We drink first and foremost through prayer. In prayer, we ask the Holy Spirit to help us, to impart to us the life and love of God. Then by faith, we thank him in anticipation for doing just that. We may, or may not, feel any different, but we believe that he will fulfil the promise of Jesus to give us living water. This asking and receiving then becomes a daily routine which over time makes a real difference.

■ PRAYER
Holy Spirit, fill me today with the life and love of God. Amen

Psalm 63:1–3 (NIV)

Spiritual dehydration

You, God, are my God, earnestly I seek you; I thirst for you, my whole being longs for you, in a dry and parched land where there is no water. I have seen you in the sanctuary and beheld your power and your glory. Because your love is better than life, my lips will glorify you.

About 60% of the human body is made up of water. Every living cell needs water to keep it functioning. Water acts as a lubricant for our joints, regulates our body temperature and helps flush out waste. It is important therefore that we drink enough water, often estimated at the equivalent of six to eight glasses a day.

When we fail to drink enough, we become dehydrated. We feel thirsty, have a dry mouth, experience headaches, lose concentration and become sleepy, even dizzy. This is why we need to drink plenty, and drink often.

When we fail to keep our hearts centred on God, we can suffer a form of spiritual dehydration. We lose our appetite for spiritual things, become lethargic in our service and perhaps find worship, prayer and Bible reading something of a chore.

The psalmist recognised such symptoms within himself, and calls out to God for his help. He chooses to remember the times he has encountered God before and decides to praise God, even though he doesn't feel like it. This is another proven way to drink the living water.

■ **PRAYER**

Lord, I am thirsty for you. Amen

Psalm 23:1–3a (NRSV)

Spiritual refreshment

The Lord is my shepherd, I shall not want. He makes me lie down in green pastures; he leads me beside still waters, he restores my soul.

Even when we are retired, life can be very busy. We can find ourselves pulled in many directions at once, trying to juggle conflicting demands. Before we realise it, we feel empty inside and our souls are dry and parched.

A priority for any shepherd is to care for the well-being of the flock. Early in the morning, he sets out, walking ahead of them, leading his sheep to the place where they can find pasture and water to drink. Then, after spending the morning grazing, they are able to rest, lying down contentedly under his watchful eye. This tranquil scene is a picture of the spiritual and emotional rest that Jesus offers his followers.

Sleep can become more difficult as we get older, with long, wakeful nights. Or we can find ourselves sleeping more than we used to. Either way, there is refreshment for our souls in making sure we get adequate rest and making space in our lives for periods of mindful stillness and silence. The soul needs such quiet moments of reflection to be re-energised and restored. This is yet another way by which we can drink the living water and be revived again.

■ **PRAYER**
Lord, I am so glad that you are my faithful shepherd. Amen

Psalm 1:1–3 (NIV)

Planted by the stream

Blessed is the one who does not walk in step with the wicked or stand in the way that sinners take or sit in the company of mockers, but whose delight is in the law of the Lord and who meditates on his law day and night. That person is like a tree planted by streams of water, which yields its fruit in season and whose leaf does not wither – whatever they do prospers.

I understand that some mature oak trees can draw up to 50 gallons of water through their root system every day, and even more if it is hot. Trees in drought-stricken areas show signs of stress by dropping their leaves early and failing to bear fruit. The tree in this psalm, however, has no such problem since it has been deliberately planted where there is a good water supply.

God's people are encouraged to be deeply rooted in him, and to do this by meditating on his word. The simple practice of mulling over key Bible verses in times of need is another way by which we can draw God's living water into our thirsty souls. As we carefully ponder the words, and welcome their truth into our hearts, we are spiritually strengthened and renewed.

Scripture meditation is a helpful practice that we can follow at any time and it will add significantly to our spiritual and mental well-being.

■ **PRAYER**
Lord, help me to treasure your life-giving word. Amen

Revelation 7:16–17 (NIV)

The hope of heaven

Never again will they hunger; never again will they thirst. The sun will not beat on them, nor any scorching heat. For the Lamb at the centre of the throne will be their shepherd; he will lead them to springs of living water. And God will wipe away every tear from their eyes.

It seems fitting that the last book in the Bible, Revelation, should point us so firmly in the direction of heaven, our ultimate destination. As we go through life, we experience many joys, but also many sorrows. In our times of need, it is important to allow the prospect of heaven to give us a sense of perspective.

One thing we know for sure about heaven is that Jesus will be there, taking centre stage as both the Lamb who makes salvation possible and the shepherd who leads us into all its blessings. All the frustrations and struggles of our earthly lives will be left behind, so there will be nothing to spoil our happiness or rob us of our joy in God.

There will no more sad tears either, although I imagine there may still be some tears of joy. Very tenderly, and with his perfect knowledge of our individual stories, God will wipe away the last of those painful tears so we will cry no more. What a prospect that is!

■ PRAYER
Lord, I look forward with growing anticipation to all you have in store for me. Amen

On eagles' wings

Lin Ball

I love the promise in Isaiah that no matter how weary or exhausted, young or old, those who wait on the Lord will renew their strength and 'soar on wings like eagles' (Isaiah 40:31, NIV).

I value my sight tremendously. But having worked for some years with people with sight loss, I find there is one particular thing I envy in my blind friends: they do not judge by appearance. Whereas I use my eyes to make easy, superficial and often incorrect assessments of people based on toned limbs, slim physique, flawless skin or fashionable outfits, my blind friends use altogether superior tools – their ears. They listen over time to what someone says and make better judgement of their real character.

'Beauty is indeed a good gift of God; but that the good may not think it a great good, God dispenses it even to the wicked.' So wrote Saint Augustine. A pleasing appearance is no mirror to either inner beauty or inner strength.

We are created in the image of God and the Master makes only masterpieces. But it's the inner beauty and inner strength of a person that's of real value. Just as well. 'As we grow old, the beauty steals inward,' wrote Ralph Waldo Emerson. However beautiful or strong you are – unless you are Dorian Gray – your looks will fade. But inner beauty and strength *can* grow with the years. How? These readings will reveal some possibilities.

1 Samuel 16:7 (NLT)

Hey, good lookin'

The Lord said to Samuel, 'Don't judge by his appearance or height, for I have rejected him. The Lord doesn't see things the way you see them. People judge by outward appearance, but the Lord looks at the heart.'

Remember the catchy 1951 pop hit 'Hey, good lookin'', written and recorded by Hank Williams? And when was the last time you saw a film – not a comedy! – where the good-looking man was the villain and a short, balding actor played the hero? Or a TV drama where the female lead was less than drop-dead gorgeous? Thankfully – due in large part to the excellence of their acting skills – we are seeing more older actors in lead roles these days. But generally, we idolise the young, strong and beautiful onscreen.

Most of us claim we don't make judgements about people based on appearance. But is that true? There have been several TV documentaries showing how an undercover journalist posing as a street sleeper or an obese person is treated differently than when he goes out in the persona of the suited businessman.

Check out the story of God's choice of David in 1 Samuel. God is always more concerned with who you are on the inside.

■ **PRAYER**
Father, thank you that you look on me with love, seeing my heart and not my ageing body or dwindling strength. Help me to look at others without superficial judgement based on appearance. Amen

Proverbs 31:30 (NIV)

Fleeting charms

Charm is deceptive, and beauty is fleeting; but a woman who fears the Lord is to be praised.

I often think that God holds a mirror up to our bodies in which we can see a great spiritual truth: that the physical is fleeting, transient. It's the invisible – personality, understanding, character – that really endures. When I meet friends after several years, I see traces of ageing in their bodies but the real 'them' is unchanged, or sometimes even enhanced by the years.

'Sarcopenia': that's what scientists call it. It's the natural process by which our muscles weaken, starting at around the age of 40 and accelerating after 75. Exercise can help, but there's no cure for ageing.

I'm not suggesting we shouldn't care for our bodies, to keep them in the best shape for the longest possible time. But, given the fact that there will come a day when the body is laid aside, no longer needed, doesn't it make sense to pay more attention to nurturing the soul – the part of us that lives forever? The soul needs exercise too.

■ **PRAYER**

Father, give me a right perspective on caring for both my body and my soul, remembering that one day I will be called to account for how I have used my time, my resources and my gifts for your kingdom and your glory. Amen

1 Peter 3:3–4 (NLT)

Inner beauty

Don't be concerned about the outward beauty of fancy hairstyles, expensive jewellery or beautiful clothes. You should clothe yourselves instead with the beauty that comes from within, the unfading beauty of a gentle and quiet spirit, which is so precious to God.

With three grandchildren, the eldest entering adolescence, I am concerned about the way young people are pressured to think so much about image. Girls and boys often experience low self-esteem and sometimes find themselves struggling with eating disorders.

I hope I can teach my grandchildren that God values a man or woman's inner beauty above all else. It's not wrong for them to want the latest designer trainers – but a healthy perspective treasures other things more. I want to tell them about the lovely behaviours that produce inner beauty – honesty, courage and selflessness, for example. And I want them to know that plain brown-paper wrapping can surround the best gift.

Novelist Leo Tolstoy wrote, 'It is amazing how complete is the delusion that beauty is goodness.' It's a lesson we need to learn at any age.

■ **PRAYER**
Pray for any young people you know, and the pressures they face to have the perfect body. Talk to God about how you can show them by your own lifestyle that you're working hard on your Christ-like character, rather than your image.

Isaiah 53:2b (NIV)

The beauty of Jesus

He had no beauty or majesty to attract us to him, nothing in his appearance that we should desire him.

As a writer, I am always struck when reading the Gospels that there is no physical description of Jesus. If I was writing his biography, I would want to paint a word picture of the man. Films that have portrayed Jesus often cast him as a physically arresting person: strong, tall, perhaps with piercing eyes or a commanding voice.

Yet the Bible is silent on the subject, except for Isaiah's prophecy suggesting he was physically unremarkable. The crowds that were magnetically drawn to him were not attracted by his film-star looks.

'Beauty is strangely various,' wrote the English writer Arnold Bennett. 'There is the beauty of light and joy and strength exulting; but there is also the beauty of shade, of sorrow and sadness, and of humility oppressed.' The beauty of Jesus was surely complex and 'strangely various' – revealed in his teaching, his healing, his love and his sacrifice.

■ PRAYER

Dear Father God, thank you for Jesus. His strength and beauty are without equal, and never clearer to us than when we glimpse his broken body, dying for us on the cross. Amen

Deuteronomy 8:17 (NIV)

All about me?

You may say to yourself, 'My power and the strength of my hands have produced this wealth for me.'

In Deuteronomy 8, we see God's perspective on the 40 years that his people spent wandering in the wilderness. It was to humble them and test their character, to find out how obedient they were (see v. 2). God had provided for their needs. Now that they were about to enter into the promised land where he would prosper them, he wanted them to remember him with gratitude and not to think that it was all by their own efforts.

In our later years, it can be tempting to sit back and congratulate ourselves on what we've achieved. Perhaps you've had a successful career; the mortgage is paid off; there are savings enough for all the tomorrows God grants us. But has it really all been by our own efforts? Our own abilities?

For a salutary lesson in the folly of amassing goods and money, read the story Jesus told of the rich man in Luke 12 and note how many times the rich man uses the word 'I'. God calls him 'fool'.

■ PRAYER

Say with David, 'It is God who arms me with strength and keeps my way secure' (Psalm 18:32). Take time to count your blessings, and give God thanks and praise for them all. Then pray for people known to you, including yourself if this is your experience, who struggle to make ends meet.

Psalm 71:9 (NIV)

Silver separation

Do not cast me away when I am old; do not forsake me when my strength is gone.

Al Gore did it at 64. Arnold Schwarzenegger did it at 65. Apparently, it's getting more common. It's called 'silver separation' – the parting of couples in their 60s and 70s often after 40 or more years of marriage. While there is a general downward trend in divorce in the UK, it's on the rise among retired people.

Disentangling two lives after decades of living together is surely challenging. While some may embrace it as a new lease of life, for others it opens up the unwelcome prospect of loss and loneliness stretching far ahead. If you have been separated or divorced – willingly or not – or if you have been bereaved of your life's partner, it's completely understandable that you might dread being alone.

Whatever our situation, there's tremendous comfort for the believer in a truth repeated in various ways throughout the Bible. 'God has said, "Never will I leave you; never will I forsake you"' (Hebrews 13:5).

■ PRAYER

Talk to God about the fears that can come with advancing years – that your loss of attractiveness or failing health might lead to abandonment and loneliness. Then thank God for his promise: 'I will never leave you nor forsake you' (Joshua 1:5).

Isaiah 40:31 (MSG)

On eagles' wings

But those who wait upon God get fresh strength. They spread their wings and soar like eagles, they run and don't get tired, they walk and don't lag behind.

My father was one of eleven children, born in an area of cramped back-to-backs in Bristol that was later condemned. Only five of the eleven siblings survived infancy and the war years. He died at 71, after more than a decade of poor health and disability, brought on largely by the poverty in which he was raised.

Prospects today are so much brighter. Better housing, sanitation, diet and healthcare have extended life expectancy for my generation and the following ones. But one by-product of living with better prospects is that we think little about ill health and frailty until it's upon us.

Poor health, when it comes, is never welcome. But the good news is that our spiritual health is not dependent on our physical strength. If we cherish our relationship with God in prayer, worship and Bible reading, there is no reason why spiritually we should not go from strength to strength.

Think of heroes of the faith such as Moses and Joshua, Simeon and Anna. The Bible gives us many stories of older men and women of God of tremendous spiritual vitality.

■ **PRAYER**

Draw me closer to yourself, dear Lord. Show me how I can grow in my faith, going from strength to strength whatever my age. Amen

2 Chronicles 16:9a (NIV)

Strengthened by God

For the eyes of the Lord range throughout the earth to strengthen those whose hearts are fully committed to him.

God is on constant watch, always alert, with your best interests at heart. And his agenda: to strengthen you. What an amazing thought.

There is a condition to that promise, though. And the story this verse comes from in 2 Chronicles is worth a closer look. Judah's King Asa 'did what was good and right in the eyes of the Lord' (14:2). He removed all traces of idolatry and established peace. When his kingship was tested by invading armies, he prayed to God for help and God gave him victory. But towards the end of his 40-year reign, he stopped relying on God. He started trusting in political alliances, negotiating by using his wealth. He met an inglorious end.

Asa's heart turned away from God and towards trusting in his own resources, despite being warned that God's strength was given to those whose hearts were 'fully committed' to him.

Do I really remain 'fully committed' and reliant on God's strength rather than on my own? A spiritual health check is always valuable, even after many years of being a Christian.

■ PRAYER

Talk to God about your commitment to him. Make a statement of intent, using the words of David in Psalm 73:26: 'My flesh and my heart may fail, but God is the strength of my heart and my portion for ever.' Amen

1 Corinthians 1:25 (NLT)

Right perspective

This foolish plan of God is wiser than the wisest of human plans, and God's weakness is stronger than the greatest of human strength.

As older people, we can sometimes think ourselves rather too sophisticated for the good news of Christ. The idealism of youth shrinks with the pressures of midlife; the shades of grey that rob our hair of colour can also rob the gospel of its vibrancy.

Tim Keller, an American pastor and theologian, says, 'We never get beyond the gospel in our Christian life to something more advanced... The gospel is not just the ABCs, but the A to Z of Christianity. The gospel is not the minimum required doctrine necessary to enter the kingdom, but the way we make all progress in the kingdom.'

No matter how mature or strong in the faith, we need to maintain a right perspective on how we really are: no less in need of a Saviour than when we first met Jesus. Even with a lifetime of achievements behind us, we still fall immeasurably short of God's standard and can find all we need only in Jesus.

■ PRAYER
Pray in the well-loved words of Augustus Toplady (1740–78):

'Nothing in my hand I bring,
Simply to the cross I cling;
Naked, come to Thee for dress;
Helpless look to Thee for grace;
Foul, I to the fountain fly;
Wash me, Saviour, or I die.' Amen

Deuteronomy 6:5 (NIV)

Living with purpose

Love the Lord your God with all your heart and with all your soul and with all your strength.

Living a balanced life is a challenge at any age. The young person often has to be persuaded of the benefits of study alongside socialising. In middle age, the demands of career dominate and spending quality time with family can be hard. In retirement, there may be more choices, but achieving a balance can still be elusive. Some are busy volunteering. Others spend time caring for older family members or for grandchildren and are often exhausted. Later still, choices narrow, limited by failing strength and perhaps fewer resources, but even then that longed-for balance can be hard to find.

Throughout our life, God's first call on our time and energy needs no justification, yet often the minutes we give to him are only the 'leftovers'.

However we've spent our lives, now is always a good time to reassess our priorities. This verse tells us where we should direct our strength – our 'all'. It's to be given to loving God. How we do that is for each one of us to discover, secure in the knowledge that our later years can be lived with purpose, with borrowed beauty and strength.

■ **PRAYER**
Help me, dear Lord, to make my later years count for the kingdom. Help me to live purposefully with the strength that you give me, and in the security of knowing that I am always – always – beautiful in your eyes. Amen

This positive, affirming book explores and reviews the meaning and purpose of our lives. As Christians, ageing gives us the opportunity to deepen and even transform our spiritual lives. *The Freedom of Years* helps those who want to undertake the journey by examining the ageing task, the inevitable changes and the possibilities of joy along the way. Read this book, see the potential and seek to age in the light of your Christian faith.

The Freedom of Years
Ageing in perspective
Harriet and Donald Mowat
978 0 85746 506 1 £8.99
brfonline.org.uk

Like the seasons themselves, our lives are variable and can change in a moment. In *Seasoned by Seasons*, Michael Mitton acknowledges this and offers Bible reflections for the variety of life's seasons: spring, the season of emerging new life; summer, the season of fruitfulness; autumn, the season of letting go; winter, the season of discovering light in the dark. What can we learn, and how can we be encouraged in each season of our lives?

Seasoned by Seasons
Flourishing in life's experiences
Michael Mitton
978 0 85746 540 5 £7.99
brfonline.org.uk

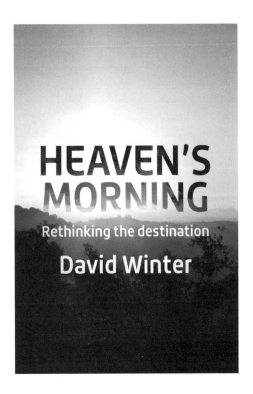

The Bible – especially the New Testament – has plenty to say about resurrection and heaven, but many Christians struggle to make sense of what it actually means in practice. David Winter's accessible book explores the biblical teaching on what happens after death and considers what difference this can make to our lives here and now. He also shows how we can present what we believe about eternity as a source of hope to our sceptical, anxious world.

Heaven's Morning
Rethinking the destination
David Winter
978 0 85746 476 7 £7.99
brfonline.org.uk

To order

Online: **brfonline.org.uk**
Telephone: +44 (0)1865 319700
Mon–Fri 9.15–17.30
Post: complete this form and send to the address below

Delivery times within the UK are normally 15 working days. Prices are correct at the time of going to press but may change without prior notice.

Title	Issue*	Price	Qty	Total
Come, Let Us Age!		£6.99		
The Freedom of Years		£8.99		
Seasoned by Seasons		£7.99		
Heaven's Morning		£7.99		
Bible Reflections for Older People (single copy)	Sep 18/Jan 19*	£4.99		

delete as appropriate

POSTAGE AND PACKING CHARGES			
Order value	UK	Europe	Rest of world
Under £7.00	£2.00	£5.00	£7.00
£7.00–£29.99	£3.00	£9.00	£15.00
£30.00 and over	FREE	£9.00 + 15% of order value	£15.00 + 20% of order value

Total value of books	
Postage and packing	
Total for this order	

Please complete in BLOCK CAPITALS

Title .... First name/initials .... Surname................................

Address ....

.... Postcode ....

Acc. No. .... Telephone ....

Email ....

Method of payment

☐ Cheque (made payable to BRF)   ☐ MasterCard / Visa

Card no. ☐☐☐☐ ☐☐☐☐ ☐☐☐☐ ☐☐☐☐

Valid from M M Y Y   Expires M M Y Y   Security code* ☐☐☐

Last 3 digits on the reverse of the card

Signature* .... Date .... /............ /............

*ESSENTIAL IN ORDER TO PROCESS YOUR ORDER

Please return this form to:
BRF, 15 The Chambers, Vineyard, Abingdon OX14 3FE | enquiries@brf.org.uk
To read our terms and conditions, please visit **brfonline.org.uk/terms**.

BROP0218   The Bible Reading Fellowship (BRF) is a Registered Charity (233280)

BIBLE REFLECTIONS FOR OLDER PEOPLE GROUP SUBSCRIPTION FORM

> All our Bible reading notes can be ordered online
> by visiting **biblereadingnotes.org.uk/subscriptions**

The group subscription rate for *Bible Reflections for Older People* will be £14.97 per person until April 2019.

☐ I would like to take out a group subscription for .... (*quantity*) copies.

☐ Please start my order with the September 2018 / January 2019 / May 2019* issue. I would like to pay annually/receive an invoice with each edition of the notes.* (*delete as appropriate*)

Please do not send any money with your order. Send your order to BRF and we will send you an invoice. The group subscription year is from 1 May to 30 April. If you start subscribing in the middle of a subscription year we will invoice you for the remaining number of issues left in that year.

Name and address of the person organising the group subscription:

Title .... First name/initials .... Surname...

Address ....

.... Postcode ....

Telephone .... Email ....

Church ....

Name of minister ....

Name and address of the person paying the invoice if the invoice needs to be sent directly to them:

Title .... First name/initials .... Surname...

Address ....

.... Postcode ....

Telephone .... Email ....

Please return this form to:
BRF, 15 The Chambers, Vineyard, Abingdon OX14 3FE | enquiries@brf.org.uk
To read our terms and conditions, please visit **brfonline.org.uk/terms**.

BROP0218   The Bible Reading Fellowship is a Registered Charity (233280)

BIBLE REFLECTIONS FOR OLDER PEOPLE INDIVIDUAL/GIFT SUBSCRIPTION FORM

> To order online, please visit **biblereadingnotes.org.uk/subscriptions**

☐ I would like to take out a subscription (*complete your name and address details only once*)
☐ I would like to give a gift subscription (*please provide both names and addresses*)

Title .... First name/initials .... Surname..

Address ....

.... Postcode ....

Telephone .... Email ....

Gift subscription name ....

Gift subscription address ....

.... Postcode ....

Gift message (*20 words max. or include your own gift card*):

....

....

Please send *Bible Reflections for Older People* beginning with the September 2018 / January 2019 / May 2019* issue (**delete as appropriate*):

(*please tick box*)	UK	Europe	Rest of world
Bible Reflections for Older People	☐ £18.75	☐ £26.70	☐ £30.75

Total enclosed £ .... (*cheques should be made payable to 'BRF'*)

Please charge my MasterCard / Visa ☐ Debit card ☐ with £ ....

Card no.

Valid from [M M Y Y] Expires [M M Y Y] Security code* [ ]
Last 3 digits on the reverse of the card

Signature* .... Date ..../......./......
*ESSENTIAL IN ORDER TO PROCESS YOUR ORDER

Please return this form to:
BRF, 15 The Chambers, Vineyard, Abingdon OX14 3FE | enquiries@brf.org.uk
To read our terms and conditions, please visit brfonline.org.uk/terms.

The Bible Reading Fellowship is a Registered Charity (233280)